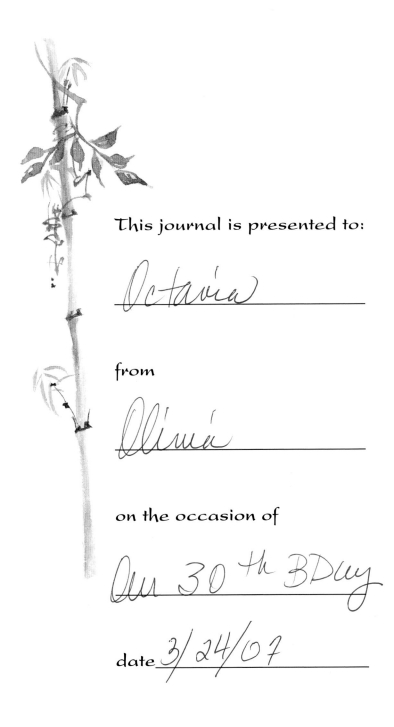

This journal is presented to:

Octavia

from

Olivia

on the occasion of

Our 30th BDay

date _3/24/07_

When giving this gift

The blank pages included in this book are the start of a loving tradition. By purchasing and giving this book, you are sharing with the recipient other women's wisdom, and by using the blank pages provided, you can add some of your own.

When receiving this gift

Other women are sharing their wisdom with you. Use the blank pages to begin a record of your own wisdom as you journey through life.

Discover your wisdom.

Share your wisdom.

Wise Women Speak

to the

Woman

Turning 30

Jean Aziz and Peggy Stout,
Editors

Capital Books, Inc.
Sterling, Virginia

Capital Books, Inc.
P.O. Box 605
Herndon, Virginia 20172-0605

Illustrations by Marie Brode

ISBN 1-892123-86-X   (alk.paper)

Library of Congress Cataloging-in-Publication Data

Aziz, Jean
  Life lessons for the woman turning 30 / Jean Aziz,
    Peggy Stout.-- 1st ed. p. cm.
  ISBN 1-892123-86-X
    1. Women--United States--Psychology--Miscellanea.
      I. Stout, Peggy. II. Title

  HQ1206 .A97 2002
  646.7'0082--dc21

                                    2001054824

Printed in China by Regent Publishing Services on acid-
free paper.

First Edition

10 9 8 7 6 5 4 3 2 1

Wise Women Speak

to the Woman Turning 30

A Personal Note . . .
How this came to be

From Jean — It's hard to buy something for the woman who has everything. It's especially hard when you want the gift to be meaningful for a special birthday. With that reality, I decided to write a letter to my daughter, Astrid, on her thirtieth birthday. I wanted to give her the benefit of my own experiences and, hopefully, some "life lessons" accumulated over the past two decades. I figured this was my last chance to give unsolicited advice about how to live her life, now that she was really growing up!

Before she even had a chance to read it, I knew that I had left out some things I had wanted to include. At that moment I realized that there were lots of women my age who probably had lessons to share with their daughters, too. The idea for this book was born: ask other women to share what they had learned since turning 30 that they would want other young women to know.

From Peggy — I have always been inspired by people's "stories," their experiences, and interested in examining issues of life from different perspectives. Since long before the birth of *Wise Women Speak* I've felt that the true experts or wise people in our society are the "ordinary" people who may not be celebrities, authorities in the field, or even well educated, but who are able to gain insight from their own lives and share it in meaningful ways with others . . . so asking women to share their knowledge seemed a very natural thing to do.

From both of us — As lifelong friends we've shared the special times and events in each other's lives. Additionally, as colleagues in the educational system we've collaborated on professional writings and presentations together. Astrid's thirtieth birthday served as a catalyst for a project in which our temperaments, talents, and vision could come together. As we create a loving gesture from many loving hearts, we are promoting the realization that all of us can be thought of as "wise women."

Why this birthday...

Similar to becoming "sweet sixteen," turning thirty is often seen as a pivotal birthday. Twenty-one-year-olds are "legal" adults; becoming thirty places you at the next stage of womanhood. No longer a twenty-something seeking the pleasures and benefits of the adult world, the thirty-something woman is establishing her profession, working toward financial independence, often married, and possibly considering motherhood, if not there already. Her focus shifts to the bigger issues of partnering, parenting, fulfillment, balance, and spirituality. She comes to recognize her desire to be a woman of self-awareness with depth and an empowered spirit.

In this new decade of your life, pursue activities that enable you to become aware of your own wisdom. This book offers you an opportunity to do so.

As a symbol for Wise Women Speak,
the Chinese character SAGE has been chosen.
Represented by images of "ear" and "mouth"
and a character for "great/ultimate point,"
the symbol suggests that through listening
to the experiences of others,
as well as their own, our wise women
gain the ability to speak about
their ultimate understanding of the universe.

Who are wise women...

Wisdom can be defined as "understanding what is true, right, or lasting". The wisdom of women in our culture is unique to each woman, yet holds a common ground, based upon our responses to experiences of special times and events in our lives. These experiences provide true, right, and lasting lessons for all women, at all ages.

Wise women are those who have lived ordinary lives in an extraordinary way. They are mothers, daughters, wives, sisters, aunts, grandmothers, and friends. They are indispensable forces in the home, community, and workplace, representing every conceivable profession and circumstance. Ordinary women become wise women once they have recognized and incorporated the knowledge of how turning points such as marriage, birth, aging, illness, and death affect their lives. What is unique is the insight developed, based upon accumulated experiences and observations at these pivotal times. This insight becomes a part of wise women's daily lives, fostering a sense of adeptness and competency as well as forming the foundation for their sharing of wisdom and knowledge.

Wise women, creatures of their own experiences and their lessons learned, provide us with an understanding of universal issues common to all women. It is this wisdom that reflects life's ultimate truths, right and lasting for women of all generations.

Discovering your wisdom...

The unexamined life is not worth living
—Socrates

Wise women and sages are made, not born. Living life without ever asking "why" or "why not" is like flying a kite and never looking up. You only see the string running out and never raise your eyes to see the beauty of flight. It all seems rather pointless and joyless when you don't look up and appreciate the magic.

Most of us strive only to get the answers. We fail to enjoy the search. Regrettably, once we have an answer, we start all over again, never realizing that what drives us is the question, not the answer. The answer gets tucked away while we launch the next search. Settling for the answer tends to create an unenlightened life with little insight about what we have really learned.

From the time of early Greek and Roman philosophers, the importance of asking questions about life's experiences has been recognized as an essential aspect of living a fulfilled life. By pondering questions, we get to know ourselves and take the time to examine the journey of our life. If we want to understand the unique joy and meaning of our own lives, then ultimately we need to think about questions such as:

What do I know now that I didn't know before?

What happened in my early life that has affected how I respond to certain situations?

What insight have I gained?

What's the best way for me to remember how to handle difficult situations?

How can I avoid making the same mistake repeatedly?

Learn to love the questions if you want to discover your wisdom . . .

Sharing wisdom...

It is our belief that down through the ages, women from every part of the world and all walks of life have been concerned with the same issues of womanhood. Thoughtful women who have experienced life's losses, joys and surprises have something to share with other women. It is in this sharing, whether through the spoken or written word, art form, or performance arts, that women help one another, providing insight and assisting in creating a more fulfilling state of womanhood.

The women who contributed to this book did so with honesty and thoughtfulness. They hope your journey will be a little easier and perhaps more enjoyable by their sharing. These lessons vary from serious to light-hearted; some are humorous, some self-evident, and some profound. We intentionally included this variety to reflect our belief that all thoughtful women have wisdom worth sharing.

Take what resonates with you and continue your journey of womanhood a bit wiser.

Never think
you have learned
all there is to learn.

— Carolyn A.

Now
is the
time
to assess
your
goals.

— Joy S.

Set high goals
for yourself
but be happy
with and proud
of what you
actually attain.

— Shelley S.

Learn
to be still
and get
to know
yourself.

— Peggy S.

Like
yourself.
Be happy
with who
you are.

— Polly D.

Recognize
your strengths,
claim your
rights, use
your influence.

— Patti D.

Follow
your
intuition.

— Donna C.

Believe in yourself
and your power
to have positive
relationships.

— Joy S.

Always
listen to
your heart
when making
major life
decisions.

— Peggy S.

It's time
to take
a moral
position
if you
haven't
already.

— Jean A.

Now is the time
to create a "life list" . . .
write down what you
wish to experience,
see, or learn over
your whole lifetime.
Recognize that these
may change as you
move through life,
but they will serve
to guide your decisions
along the way.

— Peggy S.

Charge
fearlessly
into
adventure.

— Laurie P.

Know the
boundaries
beyond which
you will not allow
trampling or
trespassing.

— Elizabeth S.

Never lose your
sense of humor.

— Marta B.

Find
opportunity
for learning
in every
experience.

— Mary M.

Know
your issues
and learn
how to deal
with them.

— Jean A.

Focusing on an issue
with negative energy
is a waste of time.

— Peggy S.

Keep
learning
to ride
the waves
of change.

— Wendy S.

Use
your heart,
common sense,
and faith
to cope with
adversity.

— Judy D.

You can
be strong
without
diminishing
others.

— Linda R.

You are
ultimately
responsible
for yourself,
so treat
yourself well.

— Mary A.

Ask for what
you need
from those
you love —
you can't expect
that they will
automatically know.

— Polly D.

If you want
someone to
celebrate your
birthday, give
them plenty of
notice about
how to celebrate
it in the way
you want.

— Mary A.

You can't
make anyone
do anything;
you can only
trust them
to do the
right thing.

— Jean A.

Trust
your instincts.
Don't be swayed
too easily
by the opinions
of others.

— Sally B.

Take
care of
yourself
physically,
emotionally,
and spiritually
—no one else will.

— Polly D.

Don't settle
for ordinary
when you
can have
extraordinary.

— Carolyn A.

Find out what
nourishes your soul
and be mindful
of what you do
to nourish
yourself.

— Wendy S.

You are your
own worst critic
as far as beauty
is concerned.
Concentrate on
and accentuate
your assets.
Don't dwell on your
perceived defects.

— Claudia D.

Remember
that how you
treat others
will determine
how you
will be treated.

— Mary A.

Get a pet
—it keeps
you real.

— Brigid D.

Remember your creator
and continue to discover
what your creator
reveals to you.

— Wendy S.

Seek creative
endeavors
—creativity is
the soul reaching
for a voice.

— Alice W.

Be generous
not only in giving
but also in receiving.

— Nayyara C.

Always
tell the
truth.

— Brigid D.

Life is a process.
Trust the process.

— Mary M.

Don't despair
in adversity.
It teaches
the harder
lessons of life.

— Jean A.

Finish
what
you
start.

— Linda R.

Resolving
uncertainty
is a process;
people do it at
their own pace,
not necessarily yours.

— Jean A. and Peggy S.

Discover
what
brings
you joy.

— Jean A.

Learn to love
your time alone
—it's the best time
to dream, hear
your heart
and tap
your creativity.

— Donna W.

Don't be shy
about dining alone
in a restaurant.

— Jean A.

Enjoy
moonlit
nights.

— Wendy S.

You may have
a plan for where
you're going,
but always
remember where
you've come from.

— Bernadette D.

Live up to
your parents'
expectations—
they deserve it.

— Jean A.

Encourage
and savor
a new dynamic
with your parents
as adults.

— Susan S.

The places you
will go are far greater
than you can imagine.
The only obstacle,
however, is what
you imagine.

— Carolyn A.

Your
friends
often
become
your
family.

— Linda U.

Gather those
around you
who enrich your life.

— Wendy S.

Your women friends
will be there forever,
so cultivate 'em.

— Jean A.

Happiness
cannot be achieved
in the presence
of hurt, fear, or anger.

— Susan S.

It takes much more
energy to be miserable
than to be happy.
It's tiring, unhealthy
and affects those
who love you the most.

— Carolyn A.

Don't be
intimidated.

— Sally B.

Be careful
not to view
new ideas
or suggestions
as criticisms.

— Carolyn A.

If you
keep repeating
a harmful pattern
you must be
getting a payoff.

— Sally B.

Remember
that whatever
you focus on
expands.

— Kathleen M.

Don't wear underwear
to bed.

— Martha E.

Take care
of your health;
bad things do happen
to thirty-somethings.

— Jean A.

Every woman
should have
her own money
saved for
a rainy day.

— Bernadette D.

Never assume that it's
someone else's job
to take care of you.

— Mary M.

Tax shelter,
tax shelter,
tax shelter.

— Judy P.

Be grateful
for any
financial
help you get,
but don't
expect it.

— Martha E.

Don't be afraid
to spend money
on yourself.

— Mary A.

Your best
investment is
in maintaining
your physical
health and
fitness.
The time
to start
is now.

— Jane S.

There are
no free rides.
Everything
has a price.

— Sally B.

Always
cool off
before
discussing
things.

— Patty H.

Never
discuss
troublesome
issues while
horizontal.

— Kathleen M.

Don't fret about
whether people
like you.

— Polly D.

Never
commit
to doing
something
you don't
believe in.

— Peggy S.

Hover over
the toilet seat
in a public restroom.

— Mary A.

Most of what
you worry about
does not happen.

— Becky J.

Don't lend
or borrow
irreplaceable
things.

— Linda R.

Finding a life partner
begins with
finding a friend.

— Jean A.

Choose a man
who loves you
more than
himself.

— Gail O.

The barometer of time
reveals who your
true friends are.

— Donna C.

We women learn
as we gather together.

— Wendy S.

Being a lady with class
is not old-fashioned.
It brings out the best
in others . . . so watch
your language.

— Jean A.

Reflect
who you are
as truly as
you can.

— Wendy S.

Never
be afraid
to speak
your mind.

— Sally B.

Goodness
comes
from
within
and from
nature
around
you.

— Judy D.

If
you
know
you're
beautiful,
you're
really
not.

— Claudia D.

Forgiveness
is important because
it heals the pain
of anger, hurt, or fear.
If we do not forgive
others or ourselves,
we keep the pain alive.

— Susan S.

The winner
in life is
the person
who gets
knocked down
and gets
back up and
back into it
again.

— Reva S.

Like it or not,
you will
recognize
your mother's
reflection
in the mirror
some day.

— Judy J.

Say
nice things
to yourself
about yourself.

— Peggy S.

Do not accept
a table near
the kitchen door
in a restaurant.

— Mary A.

It's all in the
attitude.

— Sally B.

Always ask
for a manager
or supervisor
when you truly
want results.

— Mary A.

Life
is too
short
to neglect
those
who care
the most.

— Addie M.

Don't be afraid
to love . . . the joy and
contentment you will feel
is well worth it.
Just take that moment
in time for what it is—
not all-consuming,
but a shared experience
that may be lost if you
never open the door.

— Carolyn A.

In the long run, twelve matching napkins aren't that important.

— Suzanne S.

Life is like a minefield
we all walk through.
The one thing
we know for certain
is that we'll all be hit.
The question is when
and how badly
we'll be hurt and,
more importantly,
how well we'll recover
from our wounds.

— Reva S.

Don't slip down
into cynicism.
It is the certain path
to an unhappy life.

— Maggie A.

Being
right
is not
always
winning.

— Jean A.

A person cannot
be creative unless
the child inside
is able to fly.

— Alice W.

Conquer what
scares you most.
After that
you'll know that
you can
do anything.

— Patti D.

Don't
create a set
of expectations
for others,
only for
yourself.

— Peggy S.

Work on
your own
happiness
and other
relationships
will fall
into place.

— Mary A.

Make a
difference to
someone else,
even if in a
small way.

— Maggie A.

Being kind
and empathetic
rather than impatient
and cynical makes
the world a better place
for you and those
around you.

— Jean A.

If you can read,
you can do anything.
There are books
for every chore
or task imaginable.
Get one—and then
decide to hire it out!

— Mary A.

Understand
the bridges
we women
make, each
of us taking
even as we give.

— Barbara S.

Give
more
than you
take.

— Diane R.

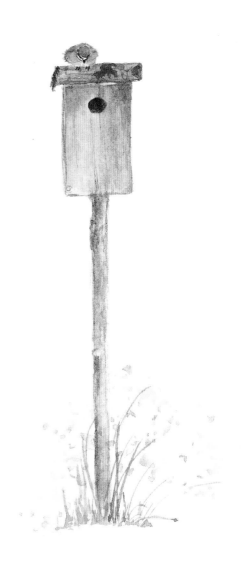

Never
let today's
worries
interfere
with
today's
joy.

— Judy P.

Your unique
talents are gifts
given to you
by a higher power;
if they're abused,
who's to say
they may not
be taken away.

— Carolyn A.

Have faith.

— Joy S.

By now you are on your way to becoming a sagacious woman. . .

Sagacious or wise women lead life in a more discerning fashion. An apt, clear-sighted approach to understanding others and yourself produces sensible intelligence. The consequences of this questioning mindset are more confidence, gratitude, empowerment, security, forgiveness, and even risk-taking. It prepares you for the future and has far-reaching effects.

Discovering your insights and following your intuition will help you travel the journey of womanhood more aware, more gracious, and in better control of the choices you make. Such learning leads to the realization that sharing encourages others, helps to simplify their journeys, and benefits those for whom we love and care.

sa·ga·cious (adj.)
wise, foreseeing, able to perceive acutely.
1. having or showing keen perception
or discernment and sound judgment,
foresight, etc.

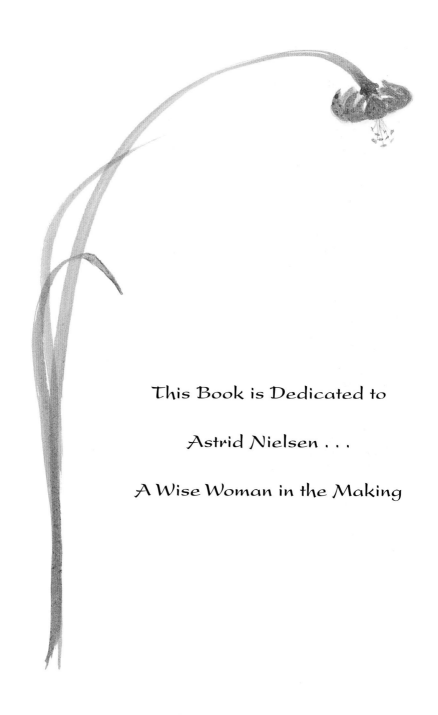

This Book is Dedicated to

Astrid Nielsen . . .

A Wise Woman in the Making

Acknowledgments

The creation of this book owes much to the many dear friends, neighbors, and family members who were instrumental in providing us with practical advice, technical expertise, light-bulb moments, vision, and, most of all, patience. They listened to us constantly talk about our ideas and were always encouraging and enthusiastic.

For their practical and invaluable advice we thank Bill and Mary Musick, Maggie Argent, Wendy Savoy, Emir Aziz, Kelly Miller, and Suzanne P. Smith.

For their time and technical expertise, we thank Jehan Aziz, Peter Blacklin, Julie Barer, Alex Roy, and Mandy Parmer.

For their creative spark and vision we are grateful to Marie Bode, Alice Webb, Susan Stacy, Jeff Stout, Bridget Bystry, and Mary Ann Wall.

For selfless contributions of their wisdom we are happy to name Gail Olinger, Linda Rollins, Kathleen Martens, Mary Musick, Judy Pachino, Martha Ellis, Judy Jackson, Shelley Stout, Maggie Argent, Wendy Savoy, Diane Rausch, Patti Drake, Polly De Hart, Bernadette Durkin, Sally Baer, Joy Stout, Nayyara Chaudhry, Linda Ulrich, Donna Castoria, Marta Binstock, Brigid Demand, Judy Donovan, Laurie Phillips, Reva Shar, Carolyn Auld, Mary Alden, Jane Sharp, Barbara Simon, Suzanne C. Smith, Susan Stacy, Elizabeth Surette, Becky Jett, Addie Miller, Patty Stout-Hrable, Alice Webb, Claudia Rowley Dailey, Donna Winterling.

And finally,
to Astrid for inspiration
to Marty and Shahid, our devoted husbands,
we are forever indebted.

Want More?
Wise Women Speak

To order: T-shirts (ecru with black lettering)

                   Accessories (mugs, canvas bags, calendars)

                   Other books in the series

                   Workbook/Workshop Information

Email us at: wisewomenspeak@hotmail.com

Read more
on our website: www.wisewomenspeak.com